Here it is, my fourth collection of poems.

I think **more bees bigger bonnets** is my best offering yet – but then I would say that, wouldn't I? It's full of politics, sideswipes at bigotry and stupidity, a good few belly laughs, and a fistful or two of dreams. And – seeing as so many of my poems are written in response to some event or other – you'll find a couple of pages at the back of the book which explain what inspired them.

My heartfelt thanks go out to everyone who's given me a chance to come and read at their poetry event, to the poets and writers who took time to read and review this book, and to all the people I've met along the way. I couldn't have done it without you.

all the best

Steve

'Steve Pottinger is something the world needs right now, a poet who looks the 21st century directly in the face. He's a writer who tempers anger and outrage with compassion and hope. He understands that, just like fury, humour is a potent weapon, and that politics and the struggle to simply live is part of the everyday for most people. It's poetry for everyman, with the language of the workplace and the pub, showing that there's beauty to be found everywhere.'

Chris Nickson, author.

'These poems are an insight into the harsh world that surrounds us. They will humour you, sadden you and inspire you; they will stay with you – I've still got *The Knock* knocking around in my head – a great testament to a great poet.'

Steve Ignorant, author and musician.

'Steve stings all the right targets, drips honey in all the right places and leaves the reader buzzin'.'

Tony Walsh (Longfella),
Glastonbury Festival Poet-In-Residence 2011

'A fellow social surrealist poet summing up the twisted values of this fucked-up world.'

Attila the Stockbroker

'These poems live in the space between high and low, between everyday down-to-earth shopping-bag reality and Arcadian dreams. Between crying and laughing. They roll, easily, like good conversation. They exist – as the title tells us – as the bees in the poet's bonnet, itches that need scratching, stuff that needs to be said. But they come to life not as diatribes but as gentle tugs on the sleeve. *Here, listen, what d'you think of this?* They're funny, too. Funny that wins an argument, funny that points a finger at the Emperor, funny that works because it's balanced by tragedy. Funny because even the humour has a point to it, a reason to live on the page, between the high and the low, the page where most of us spend our lives.'

Boff Whalley, musician, author, playwright.

'A tower block of a book, each flat contains beautifully drawn characters from 21st century Britain screaming from the windows – the girl about to have a good day, the man who challenges a conglomerate, the un-stoppable, the flawed, the irreverent, the social outlaw. This book will make you stand up as you read it.'

Joelle Taylor, poet.

They told me
I'd calm down
as I got older
but to be honest
I find that age is bringing
more bees, bigger bonnets.

more bees
bigger bonnets

Steve Pottinger

ISBN: 978-0-9932044-0-1

typeset by Steve at Ignite.
www.ignitebooks.co.uk

Printed and bound in the UK
by Bell & Bain Ltd,
Glasgow.

To have a bee in one's bonnet:
to bang on about something because it's important.

'Something better change.'
The Stranglers

'It always seems impossible until it's done.'
Nelson Mandela

Contents

The following poems were
previously published elsewhere.

on the *Poetry24* website:
Angelina
The knock
Bongo Bongo bad
Lampedusa
The ostentatious breast-feeder
You could have had kids by now
The day we elected...

in the *Morning Star:*
369 000

Let us pretend
was included in the anthology
'for the children of gaza' by onslaught press.

Others were published in collections put together
by poetry groups round the country.

Thank you all.

The girl next door

today
the girl next door knows
that something good is going to happen
I can hear her singing
through the bathroom wall

*I just know that something good
is going to happen*

today
she isn't tired
she isn't angry
today bringing up a kid alone
is something she can do
she feels it sure and certain and pure and true
because today something good
is going to happen

today
the council will fix the sticking door
the bills will come and she'll have money set aside
and she can dream her boy will never be denied
a job, because there will be jobs for all
and he'll be proud and strong
and have all the things she never got to own
because today, she knows, something good
is going to happen

today
under the grey clouds
her sun is shining
hot and bright and carrying a tune
today she is Wonderwoman, she is Supermum
a vixen, a vamp, a heartbreaker
who queues in the supermarket for reduced to clear
and dances home in the rain
because today something good
is going to happen

today
she'll buy a scratchcard
because she knows she's feeling lucky
she'll buy a packet of ten
and take five minutes out
to spark one up and watch the world go by
she'll put on the old tunes
from back in the day
and smile to herself as she unlocks
memories of lost nights, wild secrets,
love that blazed
because today something good
is going to happen

today
none of the mistakes she's made will ever matter
she'll forgive herself, go out and make some more
because she's starting out with a clean slate

she will survive
she will thrive
she feels alive in a way
she feared that she'd forgotten
and those obstacles in her way
are nothing she can't overcome
because today
hope is blooming inside her
like flowers in the desert once the storm has gone

and she is singing because
she knows, for a cast-iron
solid gold copper-bottomed certainty
that something good
is going to happen
today... or tomorrow...
or sometime when she has all
but given up believing
something good something undeniably
wonderfully good is going to happen

and I hear her singing
through the bathroom wall
and I think it already has, girl
it already has.

Angelina

Gary
never known for his subtlety
three pints in at The Anchor
half an eye still on the game
orders another lager

swigs
stands tall at the bar
and tells us all
this changes nothing
he wouldn't kick her out of bed

hilarity
he's no oil painting himself
never has been never will
shouts of he should be so lucky
in another life in his dreams

burst
of the old anglo-saxon
to put us in our place
and then the surprise
he takes a sip and asks us

imagine
the quacks went at your jewels
with a knife
to save your life
could you would you tell the world?

Gary
never known for his subtlety
three pints in at The Anchor
drinks the silence
nods and tells us

courage
looks and more balls
than all of us together that Lara
and then Gary orders another lager
half an eye still on the game.

Mum's the word

Edward Snowden's in the spare room
spies are hiding in the bin
a pack of Fleet Street's finest
are struggling to get in
there's paparazzi in the flowerbeds
and killers in the yard
And Ed thinks he's in Cuba
it's going to be hard
to explain this is a terrace
in a sleepy cul-de-sac
and it's nothing like Havana
but he'll have to watch his back
because he's made a lot of enemies
who don't owe him any favours
and the postman's looking shifty
and who the hell are these new neighbours?
That couple by the lamp-post
and the bloke up on the roof
and the pensioner at the bus-stop
and that surly hooded youth
are all people I don't recognise
the street is full of strangers
and Edward may be paranoid
but he thinks that we're in danger
of extreme and sudden termination
at the hands of agents of the state

or rendition to a lonely cell
where no-one knows our fate....
Two blokes come to read the meter
their smiles are very sweet
but from the bulges in their jackets
I believe they're packing heat
unless the Mormons have gone urban
things are looking pretty hairy
I never knew that having Ed to stay
would be so bloody scary.
The noise outside is deafening
the sky is full of choppers
and those schoolkids in a crocodile?
I swear to god they're coppers
interspersed with ninja
and some men in black on horses
are they FBI? Ed shakes his head
it's worse, they're special forces
his palms are getting sweaty
as he's peering through the curtains
and I don't know where he goes from here
his future's quite uncertain
but for now he's in the spare room
with Digestives and some tea
and if you get asked, remember –
you never heard of this from me.

Never see a nipple....

(with apologies to John Cooper Clarke)

Beheadings are acceptable, boobs are bad
the female form's fantastic but only when it's clad
we're blasé about bullying, laissez-faire on lust
but our patriarch goes postal
if the news feed shows a bust
sign on, log in, no matter where you look
you'll never see a nipple on facebook.

We've made a Faustian pact
with our morals as collateral
pictures of breastfeeding? Ugh. Not natural.
You can stick your outrage, stuff your clamour, we
refuse to rehabilitate the mammary
sign on, log in, no matter where you look
you'll never see a nipple on facebook.

We take no sides when it comes to mutilation
but we're taking the tit out of titillation
we don't care if it's your mother,
your girlfriend or your nan
topless is taboo (it doesn't count if you're a man)
accuse us of hypocrisy, the decision that we took
is that you'll never see a nipple on facebook.

Understand that we know best
we've ads for breast enhancement but – no breasts
it's a crazy world where our policy makes sense
where execution passes censorship,
but to suckle gives offence
sign on, log in, no matter where you look
you'll never see a nipple on
never see a nipple on
never see a nipple on facebook.

The knock

Should have been your boy
back from the game
bag of fish and chips
grin as wide as the Mersey
drunk on youth and sunshine
still living every pass shot tackle
settling down in front of the box
him and the old man each with a can
to watch it all over on *Match Of The Day*.

Instead, it was coppers
neighbours, friends, the sad-eyed priest
it was *sorry for your loss*
it was the space at the table
the silence, the empty room
it was the doctor giving pills to kill the pain
knowing nothing would ever bring him back again
it was your husband fallen in on himself
it was grief you thought would end you.

And it was reporters hunting headlines
papers printing tales they knew were lies
it was official cover-ups and smears
it was the start of twenty-five years
of banging on the gates of justice

demanding the truth, an apology
for what they did to your boy
and the other boys and the girls and the men
it was learning to walk on

knocking on the gates of justice
with the families knocking with you
and the clubs knocking with you
and a city knocking with you
and hope in your broken heart.

369 000

Here is a poem
for the others
who are born on mud floors
marshland and high plain
in homes of plastic and flattened tin
in spat-out estates in lands
whose time has gone
in the mewling sprawling cities
of the south and east and rising world
who tumble down out of shanty towns
looking for work and hope and food
who doss down in shop doorways
on park benches in abandoned cars
who snatch sleep on night buses and on tubes
amid the echo of gunfire
who ride the long trains north in the night
running the gauntlet of gangs, police, *La Migra*
who slip across borders soft as water
on blistered feet
and take their calloused hands
to the sweatshop, the factory, the scramble
for work at the corner of the street
who live in fear of being
denounced, detained, deported,
who will be trafficked, who will be sold

who will die before they are one year old
who will deal drugs in the barrio, the favela
who will get by, whatever
whose crops will fail
whose names will be known to no-one
but themselves and the hot dry wind
who dream, as we do

who are coming now,
an unstoppable future.

Bongo Bongo bad

So you've spilt your red wine
you've just burnt your dinner
the bills keep turning up fat
and your pay's getting thinner
your boyfriend said he was blonde
turns out he's a ginner
who's to blame? The Bongo Bongos.

The neighbourhood sucks
and your house is a slum
you were hammering nails
and you twatted your thumb
your dad's had a sex change
and now he's your mum
whose fault is that? The Bongo Bongos.

They're lazy and selfish (and probably black)
they take what we send and they give nothing back
say they need cash for food
but they spend it on crack
a pal of a mate of a bloke who drinks down the pub
heard a girl down the supermarket say
her aunt saw it happen once, so that's gospel.
The Bongo Bongos.

They're a mythical race
they don't really exist
but they're someone to shoulder the blame
when you're pissed
and you're angry and bitter
you've never been kissed
and life's just not *fair*.
Those bloody Bongo Bongos.

But don't ever think to begin to ask why
the rich keep getting richer and the poor can't get by
could it be something to do with dividing the pie?
Do you think?
Don't bother your pretty little head about that.
Just keep blaming the Bongo Bongos.

It's irrational hate that defies explanation
Aid isn't the problem, but greed. Exploitation
is why so many need food banks all over this nation
and when you're pointing the finger
in rage and frustration
and you think it'll offer you some consolation
to blame the Bongo Bongos...

you're wrongo, wrongo, wrongo,
wrongo, wrongo, wrongo,
wrong.

ginner: not a mis-print, but a dialect word for 'ginger'.

Lesson

These gated communities
cicadas chirring
calm, empty streets
are not for you.

These fucking punks are all the same
hooded tops, iced tea and Skittles
not a care in the world.
Unarmed. And dangerous.

Dead kids tell no tales
and the suburbs know that
the poor and black and young
are up to no good anyway.

Know your place.
You, and uppity Rosa,
and White House Obama
it's the back seat of the bus, boy,
in the land of the gun and the free.

No-one likes an angry poet

Next Tuesday
what with the weather being lousy
and the nights drawing in
and the rent being due
and the electricity bill hitting the floor
and going through the roof at the same time
and feeling in need of a mid-morning pick me up
to shore up my morale,
I'm going to put on my rain gear
head into town
walk into Caffè Nero
and smile at the barista.

She'll smile back
because it's good to smile
and I'll order a grande mocha
with an extra shot
with a whirl of whipped cream
and chocolate sprinkles on top
and just to get that sugar hit up and running pronto
I'll have a slab of Chocolate Crunch™
and no, I won't be taking it away.

When she sets it on the counter
I'll give her everything I have

in my pockets.
Sixteen pence in shrapnel,
three washers, one old bus ticket,
and the business card some psychic medium
keeps posting through my door
promising an end to all my worldly ills.
How a man of such prodigious talents
wasn't stopped dead in his tracks
the instant he smashed into the
I don't think so, sunshine
wall of scepticism
just inside the front gate, I'll never know,
but that's another story for another day.

Back in Caffè Nero
the barista looks puzzled.
She counts up the coins,
hands me back the washers and the bus ticket,
slips the business card into the pocket of her jeans,
smiles,
and tells me I still owe her £5.74.

I smile back
because no-one likes an angry poet
and I take a deep breath
and I tell her
that as Caffè Nero has paid no corporation tax
on its UK profits for the past two years
I reckon they owe me a couple of hospitals

an old people's home
and an upgrade of our creaking transport system.

Minus £5.74.

The barista goes to get the manager.
I take a big slurp of mocha
and a huge bite of Chocolate Crunch™
to keep ahead of the game,
and when he arrives and asks what's going on,
and knowing no-one likes an angry poet,
I give him a big chocolatey grin
and explain about the tax.
Then, before he can whip it away,
I have another gulp of mocha
grab the rest of the Chocolate Crunch™
and stuff it in my gob.

He threatens to call the police.

There's a long pause.
Partly because my mouth's so full of chocolate
I can barely speak,
but mainly because my response
when it comes
is going to be so densely packed
with fury and expletives
we can't let it loose till well after the watershed
accompanied by some kind of warning

because all this smiling is hard work
and yes, no-one likes an angry poet
but I'm a poet who loves words loves people
and believes some things
are worth getting angry about
and if you don't see the difference
between those two
then I probably lost you
soon after I put my rain gear on
back at the start.

And this is *my* poem.
And in my poem
the customers who've been in here with me
chatting, reading, sheltering from the rain,
they stand as one.
The baristas, tired of working
on their feet all day
throw their aprons to the floor
seize the takings
and march out of the door
and we make our way
from branch to branch
all through town
filing the streets
emptying the tills
into a large sack
which we deliver to the nurses up at A&E.

We hand out lattes to bus drivers,
fire espressos and carrot cake
into the mouths of homeless people,
give paninis to the unemployed.
Coffee mugs in hand,
chocolate smeared across our faces,
fired up by our belief we're all in this together
and that an injury to one is an injury to all
we storm Vodafone HQ and Amazon UK
for a quiet chat
about the money they owe us,
and as the winter sun
breaks through the clouds
and the windows of the City
are a seamless wall of gold,
I look around,
one poet in a sea of millions

and by god, we're smiling.

#foxnewsfact

Fox News got an expert in
to tell them about terror
he said he had some beans to spill
and then he made this error
if you ever needed evidence
his analysis is cracked
he told them Birmingham's gone Muslim
it's a #foxnewsfact

he's seen the Mecca Bingo halls
and put two and two together
then come up with 5, or 49,
he's really not that clever
he thinks Aston's twinned with Al-Qaeda
in a global terror pact
now that Birmingham's gone Muslim
it's a #foxnewsfact

he's sure the call to prayer in Rackhams'
rings out from New Street's minarets
the hajj happens in the Bullring
where Hezbollah have just met
with Ozzy and Black Sabbath
about laying down some tracks
because Birmingham's gone Muslim

it's a #foxnewsfact

the jihadis hang out in the sunshine
that fills Paradise Circus
there's camels at the bus stops
and the pubs are wearing burqas
the city's motto *'Death to infidels'*
has the pizazz that *'Forward'* lacked
you see Birmingham's gone Muslim
it's a #foxnewsfact

the M6 has madrassas
at J4, 5, 6, and 7
the Spaghetti Junction slip-road
is a hotline straight to heaven
and we all wear Muslamic ray guns
strapped onto our backs
because Birmingham's gone Muslim
it's a #foxnewsfact

there's sharia law and Cadbury's
a land of Dairy Milk and honey
and if today the weather's Shi'ite
tomorrow will be Sunni
and Villa and the Blues
are both best on the attack
since Birmingham's gone Muslim

it's a #foxnewsfact

the boats in Gas Street basin
are all learning the Koran
Chiltern Mainline runs from Moor St
to north Afghanistan
there's a fatwa on pork scratchings
and the priests have all been sacked
because Birmingham's gone Muslim
it's a #foxnewsfact

if the Queen visits, she must grow a beard
a man must be her minder
and she must walk five steps behind
one of the Peaky Blinders
it's nice to have her over
but we're glad when she goes back
now that Birmingham's gone Muslim
it's a #foxnewsfact

you may be thinking to yourself
can all of this be so?
Is Moseley full of mullahs
and I didn't know?
A caliphate with chips and peas?
Does such a thing exist?
Well, Fox News got an expert in.
Would you really question this?
Just sit back and gawp in horror
at a world that's out of whack

when he tells you Birmingham's gone Muslim
it's a #foxnewsfact
you see Birmingham's gone Muslim
it's a #foxnewsfact
because Birmingham's gone Muslim
it's a #foxnews

#foxnews   (#lies)
#foxnews   (#fear)
#foxnews   (#cometobirmingham)
#foxnews   (#illridewithyou)

#foxnewsfact

Keytown

I remember
all this were factories,
forges, fires, and furnaces
and you teaching me the alphabet, or sums
in a yard touched gold by summer.

Round us earth shook
with the drop of five-ton hammers
air tasted of burnt steel
men cast, cut, laboured at machines
turned out components, pressings, locks and keys.

You wielded the needle. Swift, precise
stretched me on the kitchen table
stitched my lip whole
the world was molten metal, hot as suns
all in a day's work.

We made stuff. That was what we did
and in our manufactured din
we found identity, pride, and skill.
You healed the sick,
showed us woodland, scraps of heath, and old canals.

There was beauty in the engine of the world.

Now the air here is clean, dead
smells of nothing
you are stooped and slow and old
are sick, need the healing of others.

Ragwort and willow-herb now grow in piles of brick
where once stood plants ablaze
with arc and press and lathe at work.
All gone. Yet underfoot
the faintest echoes of a trembling earth.

Give him a grid reference

Some folk like to play promoter
claim they live to put on bands*
in truth they've got their work cut out
finding their own arse with both hands.

They draw up maps and spreadsheets
they make strategies and plans
but its location's still a mystery
Where's my arse? Shit! Where's my hands?

They fight down waves of panic
they ask relatives and friends
they seek help in online forums
but their problem never ends

They've certificates from business school
their teachers said they're clever
but they haven't got a hope in hell
of bringing hands and arse together.

The concept seems so easy
the reality is glum
there's nothing worse than using google earth
to help you find your bum

Now perseverance is a virtue
but the truth is I'd be lying
if I claimed even for a moment
that I respect the fact they're trying

To overcome their inability
to have their buttocks meet their palms
if they were an infinite number of monkeys
with an infinite number of arms

They could be at it for all eternity
and it still would never happen
you could throw in MRI and CGI
and Ordnance Survey mapping

And it would make no sodding difference
they still wouldn't have a hope
of getting right what is so simple
and instead they merely grope

Round blindly in the darkness
claiming they like to put on bands*
when the truth is they've never ever once
found their own arse with both hands.

*they also say they like to put on poets, and are no better at that.
Hence the poem.

Last out of Pandora's box

The sun is always there
you used to say
there behind the clouds
waiting to break through.

I hung on those words.

And now I wish you were here
so that I could show you
how outside the rain's been falling
for longer than I remember
day after day after day
and the skies are grey and heavy
the streets run with water
the fine clothes we were so proud of
are now stained and patched with mould.

I wish you were here
because without you this town is empty
and I drink alone
hunting the echo of your laughter
finding only the bottom of the glass
again, over and over
till closing.
I want to whisper drunken secrets
in your ear, as always,

to tell you that I miss you
and that I know now you were wrong.

The sun won't be coming out anytime soon
and your words don't change that
the world is full of people lashing out
with cruel knives and sharpened words
eager to draw up battle lines
to fall back into the certainty of trenches
the comfort of old wars
wrapping themselves in tattered flags
and the blood of strangers.

I want to tell you
that today, as the rain falls
and the light fades thin,
marionettes are dancing
to sweet discordant music
blinded by silver, bought off by gold
that we have learned nothing
that I put a foot through the TV long ago
and it made no difference.

I'm burying hope
just as I buried you
in bitterness and baffled consternation
shuffling forward to nothing very clear
more from habit than in expectation
and somewhere in the corner of my eye

I see the ghost of your conviction
and your smile
telling me
the sun is always there
behind the clouds

damn you

the sun is always there.

Loneliness of the long distance fisherman

He's the master of mackerel, the scourge of the whiting
sixteen stone dripping wet, and he's going down fighting
he stares at the sea with his feet on dry land
and he plays with his spool, with his rod in his hand.
The sea bass are out there, and turbot, and ling,
but he's been here all day and he's not caught a thing
the tide's on the turn and the weather is fine
but his bait goes unbitten, there's nowt on his line
his lures are unloved, his efforts at angling
not up to the mark, his titbits left dangling
his stomach is grumbling, his spirits are low
he's got all the gear, but he's nothing to show
for all of his efforts, just a prick in his hands
from skewering worms which he dug from the sand
when he still had high hopes he'd return from the sea
successful, and laden with fish for his tea.

And he casts and he curses, alone on the beach-a
while his wife nips to Iceland, and buys herself pizza.

The ostentatious breast-feeder

Drinking in my local
last dullday afternoon
soft drizzle outside
nothing much happening
usual 21st c. sense of ennui

when the door burst open
and a woman danced in
spinning wheeling pirouetting
across the floor
up on to a table
scattering drinkers before her

eyes flashing devilment and untamed fire
the shimmer of her dress was scarlet,
silver, purple, maybe green –
when we talked about it later
none of us agreed –
and as the trumpets kicked in
with something latin
I paused, mouth open
pint in hand.
Since when had we had a brass section
in the toilets?
What did this mean?
Then I saw the infant at her breast

and I understood
this was what Nigel
had been rambling on about
the old soak.

Ostentatious? By god, he wasn't joking.

As the music swelled to a crescendo
she sprang onto the bar
stamping her heels the length of it,
one arm held aloft, defiant
head thrown back in a piercing banshee scream
a howling wail that lifted the hair on my neck
and as the child suckled, contented,
and fireworks burst along the line of optics
and confetti cannon spewed
a blizzard of paper
into the room

I was on my feet
with all the others
whooping cheering punching the air
Yeah! Yeah! Yeah! HELL YEAH!!

That night
I dreamed of gurgling babies
fat as Buddhas
and woke smiling.

Lampedusa

This is where they come from:
villages eaten up by sand
river beds run dry
lands of red earth stained with blood
where there are mobs, bombs, bullets,
crops that fail.

This is who they are:
the young, the desperate, the brave,
fathers with daughters, motherless sons,
whose sin was to be born poor
worship the wrong body
bow before the wrong god.

This is what they carry:
hope, crumpled dollars, memories of home,
slips of paper with the number of a phone
for an uncle in Milan, a cousin
swallowed in the cities of the north
who has work, who sends back pittances
and letters rare as desert rain.

This is where they place their fate:
in the hands of men with guns and easy smiles
who speak only the cold esperanto of money

who wait, patient and sure
promises tumbling from the wet caves
of their mouths
smooth and soft as water.

This is where they lie:
washed up in their scores
on the shores of Lampedusa
their souls slipping the leash
back to Africa
their dreams and their names
known only to the sea.

Ten years on

they are still too far off for us to hear
too close for us to see

in the kitchens
in the nail bars
in the empty semis
where the ganja grows
cleaning offices by night
packing trucks by day
faces we don't recognise
names we never know
figures out of focus
shimmering like ghosts
in sand and rising water

never waving, but drowning.

Leftist worldview, my arse

On days when life's getting me down
and I fear I've the brains of a bimbo
I write a wee verse
'cause it could be much worse
I could be that ****** Rush Limbaugh.

Feel free to complete the last line yourselves.
I couldn't make *hate-filled windbag* scan.

Birmingham to London by coach...

The kids are high on sugar
their dad is high on crack
ten minutes out of Digbeth
you wish you could turn back
their baby's filled its nappy
there's a foul and evil smell
you're on a National Express bus ride
with the dysfunctional family from hell.
The eldest daughter's sodcast
is ringing in your ears
she's necking vodka red bull
while her boyfriend chugs on beer
they're en route to heavy petting
with a stop in Milton Keynes
this is going to be a journey
where you find out what shameless means
their mother's wearing jeggings
the material's stretched thin
bits of her are poking out
she should be keeping in
her attempt at keeping order
is shouting *Wayne! You little ****!*
at her lad who's gobbing greenies
on the windows at the front.
Something snaps at Coventry.

54

By Rugby, you think *Stuff it.*
The daughter passes round a joint
you join in and puff it
her dad offers you a cider
he's a very decent fella
his name is Brian, he's chopping out
a fat line of Nigella
he's a lecturer in politics
his son does engineering
the daughter works in mental health
they're really quite endearing
but they like to let their hair down
when the working week is done
and now, it's Friday evening
and they're out to have some fun.
Soon you're sipping Chablis
with his sultry sweetheart Sue
she's a psychosexual therapist
who started life in Crewe
she says wine and kundalini
are the cure to all our ills
then somewhere just past Bedford
she offers you some pills
by the time you pass through Watford
you're coming up so strong
that you're flinging off your clothing
and bursting into song
the driver barks *Sit down, sir!*
in response, you shout out *Choon!*

you're chewing gum for England
and grinning like a loon
you're telling Brian *I love you.*
That's me, that's not the drugs.
I really really mean it.
then you give the bloke a hug
by the bottom of the M1
you're having the best time
you even dance to dubstep
Dolly Parton and some grime
the coach pulls into Victoria
the party doesn't end
you're making big and little boxes
with Sue and Brian and friends.

You wake up...
two days later...
In Southampton, in a park.
You don't know how you got there
your skin is pocked with marks
which look disturbingly like love-bites
there's a number on your chest
a scrawl reads
call us soon we love you xxx xxxx
your chakras have been plundered
your underpants are gone
parts of you are tender
the rest of you is numb
dressed in lipstick smears and jeggings

the material's stretched thin
bits of you keep falling out
although you tuck them in
you stumble off in search of water
you're not feeling very well
you're the victim of a bus ride with
the dysfunctional family from hell
a small voice suggests that next time
you should maybe take the train
but you know, come Friday at 5 o'clock
you'll be at Digbeth once again
because sobriety is admirable
moderation is all very well
but you're for the life of excess
on a National Express
with the dysfunctional family from hell.

Let us pretend

Let us pretend
that we haven't been this way before
too recently and too often
that this is the way forward
that it is the road to the peace
which eluded you when you sent
planes and tanks and men
into Lebanon, Ramallah, Jenin,
Gaza, Gaza, Gaza.

Let us pretend
that this time will be different
that this time will be worth it
that you can tot up the lives
of dead children and collateral families
and declare victory
that security can be measured
in flattened houses
burials and tears.

And let us pretend
that when you build settlements and walls
and criss-cross the country with roads
and stitch it with checkpoints
and cut down olive groves
and throw people from their homes

let us pretend then
that the only terrorism in town
is the anger of young men
who build rockets they can barely aim
who have no hope,
who see their homeland dismembered before them.

Let us pretend
that this tit for tat
this tit for bloody tat
is the only way
is the legacy you will leave
your children and your children's children
their children and their children's children.

Let us pretend there can be no hope
that milk and honey cannot be shared
that Israeli and Palestinian can never
live together, laugh together, love together
two flags flutter together
let us press our face to the cross-hairs
and close our eyes
and stop up our ears
and still our beating hearts
and let us pretend, Bibi,

let us pretend.

You could have had kids by now

(for Stephen Lawrence)

Teenagers,
chips off the old block,
leaving school,
marching out into the world.

Watching their dad getting by
getting on
maybe struggling
to making ends meet
like we all are.

Watching the news on the TV
reading about an inquiry
into the police
spying on an inquiry
into the police
letting young men get
away with murder
because of the colour of their skin.

Watching an old man
who looks like granddad
telling everyone – again –
how he loved you
and how his trust has gone forever.

No means... yes, Charles?

When you're playfully tiffing a Saatchi
remember: the tears that he sheds
aren't signs that he's hurt or unhappy
but of loving contentment instead.

The nose tweak which makes his eyes water
isn't cowardly, vicious or sore
but a shorthand to show your affection
which he craves. So go on. Do it more.

And the necklace of bruises you leave round his throat
are something he'll miss when they fade
but he'll comfort himself, if it's comfort he needs
with the memory of how they were made.

Because Charles knows that language is complex
that words can confuse and mislead
if you want to be sure what your love has in mind
then you have to just measure their deed.

So tiff Charlie-boy, tiff him senseless,
keep a smile on your face as he chokes
and if anyone asks what on earth's going on
reassure them
it's only a joke.

The day we elected...

... Wilko Johnson president
the sun shone.
Which was a start.
He walked into Parliament with a heart
full of honest intentions
and a Telecaster in his arms
and we were one nation under a groove
under a riff. A distinctive, choppy, furious,
down-and-dirty-and-your-momma-wouldn't-like-it
riff.

The day we elected Wilko Johnson president
the House of Commons rocked out in a way
it hadn't since Pitt the Younger's solo
on a harpsichord he'd smuggled into the chamber
during the Poor Law debate
stilled the shouting
stopped the discord dead
and became the stuff of legend.
But now we had amplification
and a lot more soul.

The day we elected Wilko Johnson president
we ditched the old national anthem
for the new. Some bloke from Canvey Island saying
Well, shit happens

80 000 people roared along at Wembley
the 5 Live commentator was still chuckling
when San Marino scored their second.
England lost 3-1.
No-one cared.

The day we elected Wilko Johnson president
we recognised that death
is just part of the cycle of life
it's what you do with your time here that matters
we're all just feathers blowing in the wind.
The Daily Mail was lost for words.
They hadn't got an editorial for that.

The day we elected Wilko Johnson president
the sun shone.
Or it may have rained.
I don't know, I was drunk for a week
singing our three-word anthem
with strangers, then with friends
watching borders become meaningless
wealth become worthless
his simple words
I don't wanna be greedy
echoing through my mind
like a Telecaster, riffing on sustain.

Kate's war
(for Kate Sharpley)

For three years now
the war they said would end by Xmas
has made the paper one unending list of names
spat out the maimed, the blind, the broken
at dawn, as barges slip along the Thames
you hear the murderous rumble of the guns
turning fields to mud
turning men to mud
turning fathers, brothers, sons to cratered mud.

Today, with all due ceremony and pomp
accompanied by monied men who stride the world
Queen Mary visits the East End to drop
fresh-minted medals
in the hands of grieving factory girls,
to proffer for their loss
cold polished metal for beating hearts
pressed shining tin for flesh that lived and pulsed.

Your role, Kate,
is to pawn back the dress you keep for best
wait in line, curtsey, say *Thank you ma'am*
accept what is offered on behalf of what is dust
dab – if you must – at your eyes with a 'kerchief
be stoic, loyal, proud.

But you, just 22,
your father dead in the mud
your brother dead on the wire
your boyfriend dead, missing,
shot for mutiny – you never knew –
you ball up your rage and your pain and your grief
throw this consolation back
shout out loud

Keep 'em yerself, if they mean that much!

At the front
a man escaping with a scratch
from the shell which takes the head clean off his pal
might give thanks, would not believe his luck
at a trickle of blood down the cheek
when death takes battalions.

No such miracle here.
While flunkies flutter round the royal wound
coppers haul you to the cells
beat and batter you, grown men on lass
because you must learn
there are limits to men's tolerance
you must learn a girl must know her place.

Released days later without charge
friends do not recognise
your bruised and bloodied face

there's no longer a job at the factory
your father is dead in the mud
your brother is dead on the wire
your boyfriend is dead, missing,
shot for mutiny – you never know –

but you cared nothing for their baubles
dipped in poor men's blood
and you told them so.

£10 million for this?

Roses are red
Maggie was blue
now she is dead
they're having a do.

They're airbrushing history
re-writing the past
Big Ben's falling silent
the flag's at half mast.

In a time of austerity
they've money to burn
for the pomp of her funeral
but the lesson we've learned

Is they secretly know
she's not loved by the nation
her grave wouldn't be safe

so they plumped for cremation.

Venue crew to a gobshite tour-manager

You come in here barking your orders
metaphorically swinging your dick
expecting we'll jump 'cause you say so
making one thing quite clear: you're a prick.

You don't really know what you're doing
so you're looking for someone to blame
pointing the finger and snarling –
get this, gobshite, we all know your game

You're out of your depth and you know it
and the one thing you don't understand
is that if you worked with us and asked us for help
we'd be happy to lend you a hand

'Cause we're all here to make the show happen
we take pride in the work that we do
there's only one fly in the ointment
one turd in the bowl, and that's you.

From the time you walked in you've done nothing
but browbeat and bully and bluster
you're less of the master tactician
more the latter-day General Custer

And I know that it's probably pointless
teaching new tricks to an old dog like you
but next time you're about to open your trap
take a look in the eyes of the crew

Then, before you start barking your orders
metaphorically swinging your dick
giving it large and shouting the odds
put a sock in it. Don't be a prick.

You ask me where I want to live, my love

it can be the tundra, a desert, a forest, a boat
high on a mountain or out on the coast
an apartment, a terrace, a van or a castle,
a tent, yurt, or igloo, it really don't matter
but it must be somewhere

where commuters stop and stand
to marvel at another sunset
and *breathe* for the first time that day
making a mental note to phone in sick in the morning
where the Daily Mail declares its compassion
knows no borders
champions the rights of asylum-seekers
elects a teenage single mom as editor
and proclaims the benefit system
is the mark of a society
not afraid to offer help to those in need
when she hears this news
Katie Hopkins looks like she's swallowed a wasp
where politicians start speeches on british values
by saying they spent yesterday watching the grace
and beauty of swallows hunting over summer meadows
and they lost themselves in it for hours
and the speech never got written
and sod it, it was worth it

and what is this nationalistic flag-waving bullshit
anyway?
and when we vote for them they say no thanks
they'd rather be watching the swallows
and why don't we crack on with sorting things out
ourselves
we're more than capable of doing it without them

it can be a farmhouse, a mansion, an empty plot
a hot-air balloon or a racing yacht
in Lundy, Fastnet, German Bight
Trafalgar, Dogger, Cromarty, yep, all right
but it must be somewhere

where we never forget we pass this way but once
and every day is another shot at redemption
where the old and the weak and the dying
are wheeled out each evening
to feel the rain on their cheeks
in case they do not live to see the dawn
and each and every news bulletin starts
with images of the miracle of birth
to remind us what we're doing here
where kids learn about poverty and homelessness
in history books and ask
Was slavery like dinosaurs, miss?
and when the teacher asks them to imagine
what it must have been like to bed down
cold and hungry and alone

Year 9 find it so distressing she has to send them out
into the playground to burn off their confusion
and over by the bike sheds
Sally gathers the others round
and makes them swear that if the grown-ups
ever invent a poverty again
they'll give them extra double maths with Mr Jackson
till they promise to behave
and then they get back to playing kiss chase
and the playground rings with screams and laughter

it can be Glasgow, Cardiff, Westward Ho!
wherever it is, and wherever we go,
north-east Norwich, south-west Ayr
hell, Hull, Halifax, I don't care
but it must be somewhere

with a bee-loud glade and a pub at hand
where we drink by firelight, sit with friends
talking laughing making plans
where we're up every morning at dawn
walking through dew watching the sun
burn the mist off the gentle flowing river
or the rain hit the windows
or the snow fall
and all this won't even cover the half of it
because we'll be lying at night on grass
under a blanket
listening to cicadas,

72

feeling moths brush against our faces
looking up at stars so numerous we can't begin
to count them
and you explain the big bang theory to me again
and I nod and say *Uh-huh* in all the right places
but we both know there's no way I'm going
to get my head round it
I just think it looks fucking fantastic
where the world is filled with music
and the symphony of silence
for an audience of millions and an audience of one
where Simon Cowell is on gardening leave,
indefinitely
where we will make love every day
in the morning in the afternoon
whenever we bloody well want to
make love with tenderness and passion
and howling abandon
and lie in the cooling sweat of each other's bodies
and want for nothing more

it can be the tundra, a desert, a forest, a boat
high on a mountain or out on the coast
an apartment, a terrace, a van or a castle,
a tent, yurt, or igloo, it really don't matter
but it must –

and you're right
I haven't mentioned house prices

or the mortgage tracker index once, my love,
and I haven't a clue whether the market
is bubbling, booming, or about to burst
but the truth is that every time I try
I feel a small part of me go belly up and die
and yes that isn't very grown-up
and no it probably isn't going to change
and all I can say in my defence
is that with a handful of cable ties
a couple of rolls of gaffa
and a modicum of judiciously applied brute force
I can fix pretty much anything
and in my world that make us quits
because it's watching each other's backs
and nurturing our abilities
and covering each other's blind spots
that makes us strong
and that has to count for something
and this is where I want to live, my love,
with you, eating impossibilities for breakfast
growing old together
with time passing so slowly we barely notice
in a world we love still more each passing day
and where, when they wheel us out
into the soft gentle rain of our last evening
the memories will jostle and tumble
over each other like water
and when we close our eyes that night
we will believe that

74

we will wake next morning
to do it all again
that we'll be laughing
and dancing
and dreaming

forever.

If you want more poems, blogs,
and news of what I'm up to,
pop along to the website:

stevepottinger.co.uk

Angelina: written when actress Angelina Jolie announced she'd had a double mastectomy.

Mum's the word: in June 2013, Edward Snowden broke the news about what US spy agencies get up to. He then disappeared for three days. Now you know where he was.

Never see a nipple: because facebook bans nipples, but videos of beheadings still get posted.

The knock: written on the 25th anniversary of the Hillsborough disaster.

369 000: written on the occasion of the birth of Prince George, for all the other kids born that day.

Bongo Bongo bad: for UKIP MEP Godfrey Bloom, who condemned aid going *to Bongo Bongo land*.

Lesson: George Zimmerman shot and killed Trayvon Martin, a black teenager on his way home. A Florida jury found Zimmerman not guilty of murder.

No-one likes an angry poet: I originally wrote this about Starbucks. But Caffè Nero avoid tax too.

#foxnewsfact: incredibly, this is a true story.

Keytown: the Black Country town where I grew up was once the home of the UK lock industry. Now it isn't.

Last out of Pandora's box: was hope.

The ostentatious breast-feeder: UKIP leader Nigel Farage spoke out against women breast-feeding *ostentatiously* in public. It's a strange world he lives in.

Lampedusa: thousands of migrants pay to cross the Mediterranean packed in small boats, looking for a better life. Many die on the way.

Ten years on: a decade after 21 Chinese cockle-pickers drowned in Morecambe Bay, thousands of people are still trafficked to the UK for sexual exploitation, domestic work, and indentured labour.

Leftist worldview... : when Robin Williams killed himself, Rush Limbaugh linked his death to his *leftist worldview.*

Birmingham to London: the National Express bus station in Birmingham *is* in Digbeth. The rest of this poem is fiction.

Let us pretend: in 2014, Israel chose to launch Operation Protective Edge against Gaza. It was pointless, deadly, and brought peace no nearer.

You could have had kids: imagining a world where Stephen Lawrence hadn't been murdered.

No means...: when Charles Saatchi was pictured choking his then wife, Nigella Lawson, he claimed it was *a playful tiff* and *a joke.*

The day we elected: for Wilko Johnson, musician.

Kate's war: the true story of a woman daring to defy the conventions and politics of her time.

£10 million: in advance of Thatcher's funeral, the cost to the UK taxpayer was estimated as £10million. It ended up being *only* £3.6million. Now they're spending another £15million on her museum. Austerity? What austerity?

So, have you calmed down
as you got older?
Or – if you're honest –
do you find you dream of bees?
Swarms of bees, and bonnets.

Ignite Books is a small, independent publisher. This book is the latest in our series which we hope puts thought-provoking, entertaining writing before a new audience. We have a lot of fun doing this, but we also survive on a shoestring budget and a lot of graft. So, if you've enjoyed this book, please tell your friends about us. You can also find us on twitter, so drop by and say hallo. And to learn more about what we do, or to shop for our other publications, you'll find our website at **ignitebooks.co.uk**

Thank you.